WHAT'S IT ALL ABOUT?

Answering the biggest
questions of life

MARTIN SALTER

What's it all about?

© 10Publishing 2014 Martin Salter

Published by 10Publishing, a division of 10ofthose.com

Unit C Tomlinson Road, Leyland, PR25 2DY

Email: info@10ofthose.com Website: www.10ofthose.com

ISBN: 978-1-909611-53-5

Reprinted 2014 and 2016

All rights reserved. Except as may be permitted by the Copyright Act, no part of this publication may be reproduced in any form or by any means without prior permission from the publisher.

Unless otherwise indicated, all Scripture quotations are taken from the Holy Bible: New International Version.

Copyright © 1973, 1978, 1984 by International Bible Society.

Designed by Mike Thorpe / www.design-chapel.com

Printed and bound by CPI Group (UK) Ltd, Croydon, CR0 4YY

CONTENTS

INTRODUCTION

As I write this, the 2012 US presidential election has just finished. Obama has his four more years. The Republicans are licking their wounds and trying to figure out what went wrong. As I watched the *Newsnight* analysis with Jeremy Paxman and his superior-sounding friends I was struck by their breakdown of where the Republicans lost the election. A man with a particularly fine beard boldly proclaimed that it was simply because the Republicans are too religious.

As a Christian church leader, that fascinates me. Implied in his statement is the notion that Republicans are 'religious' and Democrats aren't. Yet the more I think about it, the more I think this cannot be right. All human beings have ways of answering the biggest questions of life; ways of making sense of the world; ways of ordering their lives according to a set of principles and values. It is the answers to such big questions as 'Where do I come from?', 'What am I here for?' and 'Where am I going?' which affect our thoughts and behaviours. Many of these things are based on what we *believe*.

Of course, we might not like formal religion as such, but all of us have a way of understanding the world, which shapes our values and actions. It is this perspective which some call faith, others religion, others common sense. It is these commitments which affect each and every one of us, such that it would be bizarre to claim that one political group is 'religious' while the other is not. No, they're both working from ultimate commitments about the meaning and purpose of life.

The revelation of the *Newsnight* post-election analysis is that many people are simply unaware that they operate under such commitments, and many haven't stopped to seriously think through their own world-view. The six questions that follow are designed to help you begin to do just that.

> **All human beings have ways of answering the biggest questions of life.**

1
WHERE HAVE WE COME FROM?

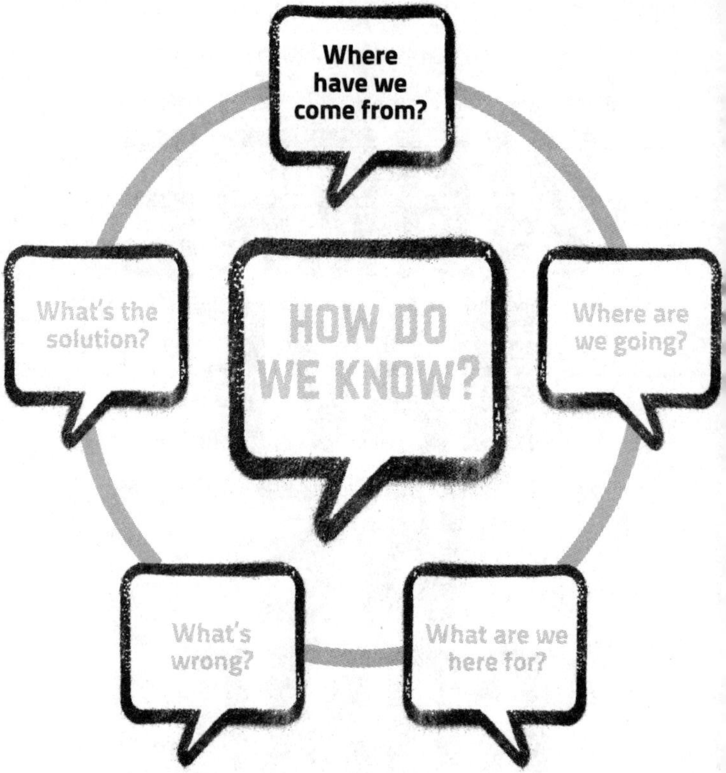
Where have we come from?
What's the solution?
HOW DO WE KNOW?
Where are we going?
What's wrong?
What are we here for?

That's the first great question to wrestle with. Where do the origins of humanity lie? Are we bags of chemicals and atoms sloshing around, the result of billions of years of random collisions and interactions of particles, birthed from some primordial gaseous mess which bought itself into existence, and subsequently birthed us also? Or are we the result of an alien experiment at colonization? Or was there a grand designer – who with intelligence and creativity bought forth a universe with a habitable earth, who created mountains, rivers, animals, stars and finally humans as the pinnacle of creation?

Many today think that modern science has buried God. The Big Bang explains where it all started, and evolution explains how we got here. Therefore, with all explained, there's no need for a creator God any longer. But here's the thing – the missing link, if you will, in the evolution of the argument: It still doesn't really answer the origins question. Bear with me. Let's suppose the Big Bang

Where do the origins of humanity lie?

theory is correct. You still have to consider where the stuff and energy came from that caused it. And if you could answer that, I'd ask you, 'But where did *that* come from?' We could spend hours doing this, or we could just admit that really, in all honesty, science cannot answer that question.

Think of it this way. My family and I enjoyed a summer holiday a few years ago in a friends' mansion. Buried in deepest Surrey, this house had remote-controlled 10ft-high front gates, stables, a tennis court, ride-on mower, and kitchen to die for. It was wonderful and huge and delightful. I don't know if my friends will ever read this, but I confess I spent a good amount of my time exploring this cavernous dwelling. There were rooms and cupboards and passageways at every turn, and being more than a little nosy, I explored. I would then excitedly report to the family what new amazing thing I'd found.

> I spent a good amount of my time exploring this cavernous dwelling.

Without wanting to be patronizing, that is the essence of science — rooting round in God's sock drawer and telling the rest of us what's been found and why it's cool (just for the record, I didn't root round in anybody's underwear drawer – honest). Obviously it's a bit more complicated than that, but in reality science and God aren't opposed. The scientist explores the universe and discovers, describes and explains all the amazing intricacies of what's there.

Evolution too only explains so much. While it is possible to demonstrate that a man is 98 per cent chimp, it's the 2 per cent that's really interesting. American historian Carl Becker said humans are 'little more than a chance deposit on the surface of the world, carelessly thrown up between two ice ages by the same forces that rust iron and ripen corn.'[1] American jurist Oliver Wendell Holmes said, 'When one thinks coldly I see no reason for attributing to man a significance different in kind from that which belongs to a baboon or a grain of sand.'[2] Professor Stephen Hawking said, 'the human race is just a chemical scum on a moderate sized planet.'[3]

Then again C.S. Lewis said, 'There are no ordinary people. You have never talked to a mere mortal. Nations, cultures, arts, civilizations – these are mortal, and their life is to ours as the life of a gnat. It is immortals whom we joke with, work with, marry, snub and exploit...' [4] And G.K. Chesterton in his book *Orthodoxy* wrote:

> **If you begin to look at beasts and men then . . . you will observe that the startling thing is not how like man is to the brutes, but how unlike he is. It is the monstrous scale of his divergence that requires an explanation . . . That an ape has hands is far less interesting to the philosopher than the fact that having hands he does next to nothing with them; does not play knuckle-bones or the violin; does not carve marble or carve mutton.** [5]

Here are some often cited statistics. If our home, earth, was even a tiny bit closer to the sun, we would burn up. Any further away, we would freeze. It is exactly the right distance from the sun at 93 million miles away. The speed at which the earth travels around the sun is just right too – at about 66,000 miles an hour. Any faster and it would be an icy wasteland. Any slower and it would be pulled towards the sun and we would

If our home, earth, was even a tiny bit closer to the sun, we would burn up.

burn up. If the force of gravity were different by one part in 10,000 billion billion billion, life on earth would be unsustainable. Of course, it could all just be a giant fluke – or it could be designed. You have to decide which you think seems more reasonable to believe.

You might fire back, 'But who made God?', to which I'd reply that it seems easier to believe God has no origin than to conceive of creation and humanity coming from nothing.

This stuff really, really matters because how you answer that question affects how you answer the rest.

NOTES

1. Carl Becker, *The Heavenly City of the Eighteenth-Century Philosphers* (New Haven, CT: Yale University Press, 1955).

2. Oliver Wendell Holmes, *Holmes-Pollock Letters 2* (ed: Mark de Wolfe Howe; Cambridge, MA: Harvard University Press, 1946).

3. Stephen Hawking, 'Reality on the Rocks', *Beyond Our Ken* season 1, episode 3, 1995.

4. C.S. Lewis, *The Weight of Glory* (San Francisco, CA: HarperOne, 2009).

5. G.K. Chesterton, *Orthodoxy* (New York, NY: Bantam Doubleday Dell, 1996).

2
WHERE ARE WE GOING?

'When you're dead, you're dead', my old grandma used to say. The body rots, the worms feast, that's it. No heaven, nothing to live or die for. Except I don't think many people believe that – not really. A friend of mine was talking recently about his grandfather's burial wishes. His grandfather lets all of his family and friends know he's an atheist, and yet he really doesn't want to be buried. Instead he wants to be cremated and have his ashes scattered over a piece of land owned by the family so that he 'can be free'. He doesn't believe there's a God but he does believe that claustrophobia might affect him post-mortem if buried.

When it comes to funerals, I've never been to one where the family doesn't have some sort of prayer, or where there is some mention of the deceased being in heaven, or waiting, or on the other side, or still with us, or in the next room. At the memorial service for the children who died in the Dunblane massacre in 1996, Lorraine Kelly read a poem by Eugene Merryman entitled 'Little Child Lost' which went like this:

Human beings seem to have eternity planted in their hearts.

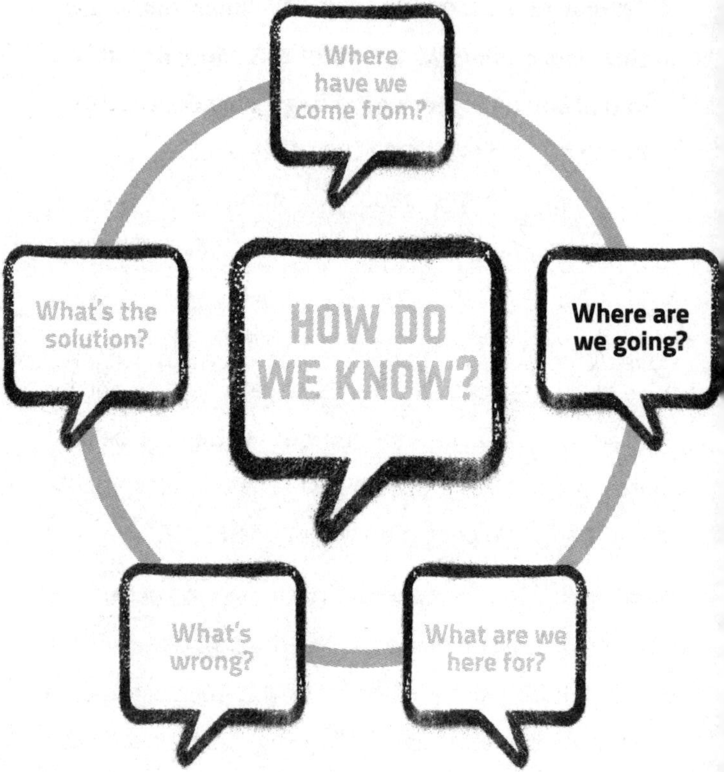
Where have we come from?
What's the solution?
HOW DO WE KNOW?
Where are we going?
What's wrong?
What are we here for?

"Although you may not always hear them, as they move upon the wings of the wind, nor may you always see them, as they go past on a ray of sunlight. Be assured they are with you."

Human beings seem to have eternity planted in their hearts so that our default position (until someone argues it out of us) is that death is not the end. People have different views on this – some believe in Nirvana; others, reincarnation; lots believe in heaven – but all of us have a sense that when a loved one leaves us, or when it's our time to go, death will not be final. Shelley, an atheist and poet, wrote in his memorial for his great friend, the young poet Keats, 'Peace, peace! He is

Not many people are willing to affirm that death is the end.

not dead, he doth not sleep – He hath awakened from the dream of life.' When it comes to the crunch, not many people are willing to affirm that death is the end. People even hold elaborate burials for dead pets.

It's a difficult one to prove either way, isn't it? Of course, there are the dubious 'I saw the light' back-from-the-dead tales, but how can we really know what lies beyond the grave? It's a bit like the prospect of a day trip to a seaside resort – I'd need someone to go and come back to tell me what's there. Yet surely what we think about the life ever-after affects in some way the life in the here-and-now?

3
WHAT ARE WE HERE FOR?

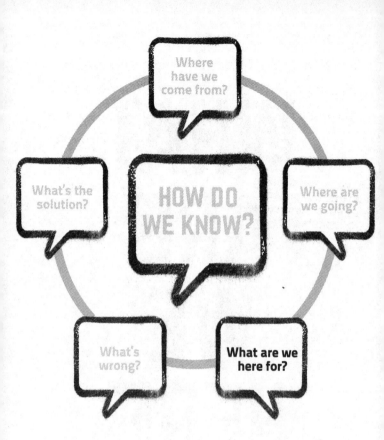

Leo Tolstoy said, 'The sole meaning of life is to serve humanity' [1] and Arnold Schwarzenegger said, 'The meaning of life is not simply to exist, to survive, but to move ahead, to go up, to achieve, to conquer.' [2] Even

Unless you assume a God, the question of life's purpose is meaningless.

smartphones have an opinion. Ask Siri on your iPhone and this is what you get back: 'Try and be nice to people. Avoid eating fat. Read a good book now and then.' The Dalai Lama said once that life's purpose is to be happy; on another occasion he said it was to serve others. But which is it? And what if serving someone else comes at the expense of my happiness? Perhaps my purpose isn't to read the Dalai Lama – he's making me unhappy.

Perhaps most striking is atheist Bertrand Russell's view: 'Unless you assume a God, the question of life's purpose is meaningless.' [3] Get that. If you don't believe in God, your life's purpose is a meaningless concept. You might as well do whatever takes your fancy – watch sports all day, eat junk food, engage in meaningless sex with strangers, do drink, drugs, Pilates or the garden, or commit any number of the military atrocities that have happened in the last hundred years. None of it *means* anything. None of it counts for anything. It's pointless, meaningless, purposeless, futile and fruitless. Yet most of us don't really live consistently with that view. Most of us have a sense of purpose – a sense that we're here for something. We're just not always sure what that something is. I've sometimes sat on the Tube in London at rush hour (that's a lie – I'm normally standing with my cheek pressed into someone's warm, moist armpit) and wondered, 'Why do you do it?' What would possess a sensible human being to play this game every day for years or decades? They certainly don't seem to be enjoying it much. Maybe one day I'll ask someone. I suspect the answers lie around a sense of purpose. It might be the desire to achieve – to climb the career ladder, make money and enjoy the finer things in life. It might be a sense of fulfilment in the task – working for a charity which improves others' lives. It might be a desire to provide the best life you can for your children.

Most of us have a sense of purpose – a sense that we're here for something.

I don't suspect that many people live life consciously devoid of purpose. And I don't think merely biological explanations for our behaviour really capture the emotional richness of our sense of purpose. I reckon most of us have an inbuilt sense that we exist for a reason. It might be as simple as providing for the kids or as profound as seeking a solution to global poverty. It's not always easy to pin down concisely what it is we think we're here for, but fundamentally we'll either think we're here for a purpose or we're not.

I reckon there's an inbuilt sense in most of us that we exist for a reason.

Which one are you? And what are you here for?

NOTES

1. Leo Tolstoy, *The Kingdom of God is Within You* 1894 (Seaside, OR: Rough Draft Printing, 2010).

2. http://www.brainyquote.com/quotes/quotes/a/arnoldschw146561.html (accessed 30 May 2013).

3. http://www.allaboutphilosophy.org/atheism-quotes-faq.htm (accessed 10 June 2013).

4
WHAT'S WRONG?

On a Saturday I buy a newspaper – normally just for the TV guide and sports pages. Recently my newspaper ran the headline 'The Sickest Mum in Britain'. It was telling the sad story of a mother who received £85,000 in benefits for falsely claiming that her son had cancer. Apparently she shaved his head and eyebrows and pushed him round in a wheelchair because she wanted or needed the money. Is what she did wrong? And who says? And where did we get this idea of right and wrong from? Is morality just a tool of the tabloids to sell more papers? Is there anything seriously wrong with the world or the human race? And if so, what?

Depending on your tabloid of choice, you may believe that what's wrong with the world is benefit cheats or immigrants or bankers or celebrity sex offenders or Catholic priests. Personally I'm almost convinced it's traffic wardens, tax men and call centres, with white van drivers close behind. It's always somebody else, isn't it – some twisted or perverted or malicious human being ruining it for the rest of us. Whatever the problem is, it's not me, it's them. But what if

Where did we get this idea of right and wrong from?

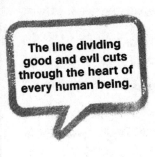

The line dividing good and evil cuts through the heart of every human being.

the problem with the world is something like global warming caused by humans? That seems to implicate *all* of us. Perhaps it pays not to ask too many questions and probe too deeply. It may be that we're all, to some degree or other, tied in to the kinds of problems which face our world.

Alexander Solzhenitsyn was a Russian writer and campaigner who raised awareness of the forced labour camps in the former Soviet Republic. He once said:

> *If only there were evil people somewhere insidiously committing evil deeds, and it were necessary only to separate them from the rest of us and destroy them. But the line dividing good and evil cuts through the heart of every human being. And who is willing to destroy a piece of his own heart?* [1]

Famously *The Times* once ran a piece asking readers to write in and tell them what was wrong with the world. G.K. Chesterton wrote in the shortest letter, simply writing, 'Dear Sirs, I am'.

Now of course, if you're a dyed-in-the-wool atheist then nothing is wrong at all, really – ultimately, I mean. There is no grand purpose or absolute moral authority. There is no end for which we were created, so all moral constructions are simply that – human constructions to help us get on. So, speaking in ultimate terms, there's nothing wrong, nothing broken and nothing which needs to be fixed. Philosophically it's consistent, but it understands nothing of the human condition.

As I write this, a young female Indian medical student has just been buried. She was 23. She was travelling with her boyfriend on a bus when a gang of men attacked them. They all raped her repeatedly for over an hour. They then beat her with iron bars. Finally they threw her from the moving bus. Two days later she died. If that's not ultimately, objectively, always morally wrong, then it's hard to say what is. But who says? And where do we get this idea from? And who, ultimately, will make the perpetrator pay? Surely there must be some final accounting for evil?

> Of course, if you're a dyed-in-the-wool atheist then nothing is wrong at all.

When the Serbian war criminal

When asking what's wrong with our world we have three options – nothing, them or me.

Slobodan Milosevic died before his trial for war crimes finished, the judge famously said: 'We express our regret at his passing. We also regret that his untimely death has deprived not only him but indeed all interested parties of a judgement . . .' [2] Really? Is there no way in which he will ever have to face the consequences of his actions?

When asking what's wrong with our world we have three options – nothing, them or me. The first seems unimaginable, the second slippery and the third uncomfortable. So which is it?

NOTES

1. Aleksandr Solzhenitsyn, *The Gulag Archipelago 1918–1956*, Part 1: The Prison Industry, chapter 4: 'The Bluecaps' (trans: Thomas P. Whitney; London: Collins, 1974), p. 168.

2. http://www.zcommunications.org/the-death-of-slobodan-milosevic-by-david-peterson (accessed 10 June 2013).

5
WHAT'S THE SOLUTION?

So, if you think there's a problem, what's the solution? How do we fix what's broken and clean up the mess?

I have three young kids. They're particularly good at staining clothing with anything from food to felt-tip to bodily fluids. Whenever this happens, they come out with something of a catchphrase in our house: 'It's OK, we'll give it to the stain-angel'. The stain-angel, I should explain, is my mother-in-law. She can get stains out of anything. We call her the stain-angel (among other things) because we thought stain-devil was a little unkind. We don't know what she does or how she does it, but she finds ways where others have failed of getting stuff clean.

Is there such a magic bullet (a stain-angel if you will) for the world's problems? If so, what or who is it?

> **Is there a magic bullet for the world's problems? If so, what or who is it?**

Perhaps it's rounding up the criminals and putting them on a desert island. Perhaps Big Brother-style CCTV on every individual might keep us in line. Perhaps it's cancelling Third World debt. Campaigns such as Make Poverty History are aimed at fixing major problems

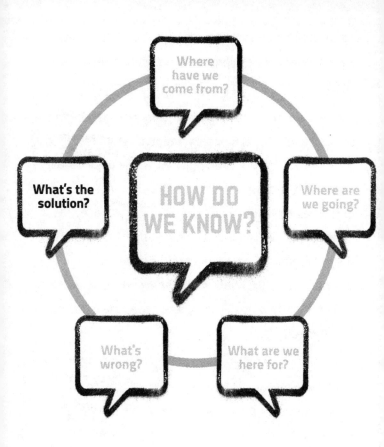

of injustice in our world. Or perhaps the solution is radical philanthropy. Comic Relief or Sport Relief raises millions every year to help with all sorts of distressing situations. Bill Gates is basically a one-man relief project, giving millions to various activities in Africa aiming to eradicate disease and famine. Maybe the solution is political – a

particular ideology or political party. It seems every time an election comes round the parties promise that this time they will bring real solutions and real change. Their election stands or falls on whether we think they really can deliver. It used to be thought that Communism would sort all the issues out; today it's free market democracy. Results so far show we still haven't found what we're looking for.

Perhaps education is key – educating people about the various problems of the world will enable the next generation to do a better job of fixing them than we have. Maybe a combination of approaches is in order. I'll leave you to decide how to mix that particular cocktail.

The trouble with all of the above is that none of them have come even close to solving the sorts of problems they're addressing. Crimes are still committed; injustice is still rampant; wars still rage; children still die of disease and famine; politicians still disappoint. Perhaps there is no real and lasting solution – what will be will be. Most of us aren't content with that, though – most of us want to be part of something that will make a difference, and believe that remaking a broken world is more than simply a pipe dream.

6

HOW DO WE KNOW?

Where have we come from?
What's the solution?
HOW DO WE KNOW?
Where are we going?
What's wrong?
What are we here for?

Here's the biggest question of all. Everyone will have different ways of answering the previous five questions, but this one's the kicker. How do you know what you think you know? That's deep. That question drives philosophers insane. How do you know where we came from, or what we're here for, or where we're going, or what's wrong or what's the solution? The philosopher René Descartes famously wrestled with this problem, questioning whether he could even be sure that he existed. Eventually he concluded that the very fact of his thinking meant he must exist: 'I think, therefore I am'.

But how do you know that there's nothing beyond the grave? How do you know we're not part of some alien experiment? How do you know we're not in some sort of Matrix dream world, having our energy farmed by machines? And how would you know there's nothing to live or die for?

How do you know that there's nothing beyond the grave?

I guess there are a number of contenders in trying to answer this question. First, you could opt for wanting positive evidence of something. If there's no positive evidence, you're not going to believe it. There's no evidence for little green men or life after death – no one has ever run a scientific experiment to prove the existence of these things, so perhaps it's better to believe that absence of evidence is evidence of absence. Another philosopher, A.J. Ayer, argued in this vein – things can only be said to be meaningful if they're true by definition or can be verified empirically. Of course, the obvious problem is that this view itself cannot be true by definition or verified empirically so cannot on its own terms be meaningful.

> **What if the herd in another place or another era think different – what then?**

Secondly, you could simply follow the herd and believe what most people seem to believe. It keeps you from offending too many people and losing friends, and if so many others think it then it must be right – yes? But what if the herd in another place or another era think different – what then? Who's to say your herd is right and theirs is wrong?

Thirdly, you could opt for your own sense of the way

things are – some kind of intuition or feeling, trusting your instinct or senses. If you *feel* like your purpose is to save the trees then who's to argue you're wrong and they're right?

All of this feels like it just doesn't cut the mustard.

Let's try a thought experiment – one posed 2,500 years ago by one of the greatest philosophers, Plato. Imagine that human beings are stuck in an underground cave. We were born there, we live there, we've never left there. We've really no idea of what's outside the cave. A fire in the cave causes shadows to appear on the wall but that's all we really see – shadows of real things. We can speculate and fight all we like about what's outside the cave, but how can we ever really know? Plato's answer was that someone needed to escape the cave – to go up to the light and tell us all the true nature of things. Maybe. But there seems to me to be a couple of problems here.

> Plato's answer was that someone needed to escape the cave – to go up to the light.

First, everyone's account of 'the world out there' is different. If Plato was right, why can't anyone agree as to what lies outside the cave? It's like six blind men groping an elephant. One grabs the trunk and declares he's holding a snake, another grabs a leg and declares it to be a tree, and yet another grabs the tail and thinks he's holding a rope. The fact is they're all wrong. Even more problematic: Who gave us the vision to see they're all wrong?

Secondly, it takes more than leaving the cave to find out what's beyond the universe. Plato's allegory only speaks about what's outside the cave, but provides no

Who gave us the vision to see they're all wrong?

explanation for the existence of the world beyond. It just pushes the question back a stage – where did that world come from? For it to really work you'd have to escape that world and find its creator or origin. But the idea of a NASA mission to escape the universe doesn't seem very likely anytime soon, so is there another way?

FOR WHAT IT'S WORTH

All these questions are designed to make you think. The answers you give to these sorts of questions reveal what your ultimate commitments are – your belief system, if you like. The question is, do you have thought-through answers to the biggest questions of life? Have you ever stopped to think about how the answers might determine the shape and direction of it? As Socrates said, 'The unexamined life is not worth living . . .' That sounds harsh, but if you're not going to wrestle with the biggest questions, what hope is there of facing the greatest challenges?

> The question is, do you have thought-through answers to the biggest questions of life?

I've spent a fair bit of time over the years trying to think through some of these questions. I'm a Christian. I'm a church leader. And I often end up in discussion about just these sorts of things.

For what it is worth, here's how I answer the six questions.

1. WHERE HAVE WE COME FROM?

In the beginning God made everything, including our first parents, Adam and Eve. He created our world and in love continues to sustain it. He gives us life and breath and all good things to enjoy. He made mountains and mice, waterfalls and warthogs, oceans and Orion, the sun and the stars. He made us in His own image. He knit us together in our mother's womb. He knows how many hairs are on our heads. He knows when we rise and when we sleep. He knows everything about us. We are fearfully and wonderfully made. And He loves us more than we could comprehend. Nobody created God – He is the one who does not need to be made. He is the Giver and Sustainer of all life. We don't know all the details of exactly how He did it, but we do know that what He created was originally very good. All the beautiful details and intricacies of our vast universe – and our earth; just the right distance from the sun, going at just the right speed, having just the right conditions for life – that's no accident. God did that.

2. WHERE ARE WE GOING?

One day God will make all things new. His original and perfect creation will be restored and made more stunning than words could fully describe. All humans are destined to stand before His perfect and just judgement seat. We will either spend eternity in the paradise of the perfected creation with Him, or apart from His love and kindness in what the Bible calls hell. Our eternal destiny depends not on our good deeds (or lack of), but our relationship to Him.

3. WHAT ARE WE HERE FOR?

God made us to be in a relationship with Him as our Maker and our heavenly Father. We're to enjoy Him and thus bring glory to Him for ever. He gave humans the task of stewarding the creation – caring, nurturing, providing. We're to be part of His work to remake our broken world with its broken people and to enjoy the new heaven and new earth. We're to live lives which honour Him, and love our neighbours, and seek human flourishing. God says you don't get to live how you want, but He does offer life to the full, with real purpose and significance that will echo down into eternity.

4. WHAT'S WRONG?

Ever since our first parents, Adam and Eve, decided to do things their own way, all of us have followed in the family business. Each one of us takes the crown off God's head and puts it on our own. We decide what's best; we rule our lives; my way or the highway. This is what the Bible calls sin. Sin isn't eating too many chocs at Christmas; it's not how many Slimming World points you're allowed – it's an attitude of rebellion which puts me at the centre and God at the periphery. This attitude has affected everything in our world. Murder, stealing, greed, lying, cheating, gossiping – you name it. If it sucks – we did it. It's no good pointing our fingers at everyone else

The sin problem is what's wrong with our world. And at the centre of SIN is 'I'.

because three more point right back at us. The sin problem is what's wrong with our world. And at the centre of SIN is 'I'.

5. WHAT'S THE SOLUTION?

How could a problem as big as that be dealt with? Certainly not by us pulling ourselves up by our bootstraps. So that's that, then.

Not quite. The truth is God came Himself to clear up our mess. God the Son in human flesh – the man Jesus Christ – came to deal with the penalty and power of sin. In His death He took the punishment you and I deserve. I deserve to face God's anger; I deserve to die; Jesus took it for me, as my substitute.

When we turn to Him for forgiveness, making Him Lord of our lives, He sends His Holy Spirit to break the power sin holds over us, and to help us live a life of obedience pleasing to God. And one day Jesus will return again to throw out the presence of sin from our world completely.

The solution isn't my performance; it's Christ's performance.

The solution isn't my performance; it's Christ's performance. Only He is able and worthy to rescue us from a terrible future.

6. HOW DO WE KNOW?

How do I dare to claim all these things? How could I possibly begin to know?

Remember Plato's cave? How would we know anything truly – unless . . . unless someone came *in* from outside the cave to tell us about ultimate realities? That's the claim Jesus makes. He claims to have come into our world to tell us about the meaning of life, our origins, ends and purpose, what's wrong and where the solution lies. He lived the perfect life and died the perfect death. He was raised from the dead and over five hundred people were eyewitnesses to the fact. The unique claim of Christianity is not that some holy human met God, but that a holy God met humanity. That's surely a claim worth considering.

If you want to find out more about the Christian faith, you have questions, or you want to become a real Christian then please contact us via email: more@10ofthose.com

Or visit www.christianityexplored.com

10 Publishing
a division of 10ofthose.com

10Publishing is the publishing house of **10ofThose.com**
It is committed to producing quality Christian
resources that are biblical and accessible.

www.10ofthose.com is our online retail arm selling
thousands of quality books at discounted prices.
We also service many church bookstalls
and can help your church to set up a bookstall.
Single and bulk purchases welcome.

For information contact: **sales@10ofthose.com**
or check out our website: **www.10ofthose.com**